The Cathedral

Including Holy Island *and* The Steps.

Daniel Janes

Collected Religious Poems

1985-2014

COPYRIGHT

Copyright @ Daniel Janes 1985-2015.

All rights reserved. This book or any portion thereof
may not be reproduced or used in any manner whatsoever without the express
written permission of the publisher except for the use of brief quotations in a
book review.

Printed by Amazon in various countries according to the origin of order.

First Printing, 2014

ISBN-13:978-1503156098

ISBN-10:1503156095

All enquires to danieljanesbooks@gmail.com

Contents

REQUIEM FOR A BOY CHORISTER. 8

LIBERATION 9

EVENSONG, YORK MINSTER 11

THE SOUL OF THE PREACHER 12

THE BLUE BELL 14

"DORIAN" TOCCATA AND FUGUE IN D MINOR BVW 538 15

BEAUTUS QUI INTELLEGIT 16

I WAS GLAD 17

   Part One 17

   Part Two 18

   Part Three 19

   Part Four 19

THE CATHEDRAL 21

   1 The Regimental Chapel 21

   2 The Path above Arches 21

3 The Aisles 22

4 The Ventilation 22

5 The Porch 23

6 The Lady Chapel 23

7 The Porch (ii) 23

8 The Screen 24

9 The Bishops Chapel 24

10 The Quad 24

11 The Psalter in the Pew 25

12 The Vestry 25

13 The Baptistery 26

14 The Treasury 26

15 The Choir Stalls 27

16 The Choir Stalls (ii) 27

17 The Vergers Pew 28

Notes on 'The Cathedral' 29

CONFUTATIS REQUIEM 30

CONFUTATIS REQUIEM REVISITED : GRIEF UNDESERVED. .31

"PROVE ALL THINGS, HOLD FAST TO THAT WHICH IS GOOD" 34

EVERY MAN 'NEATH HIS VINE AND FIG TREE. 36

CATCH A DEVIL ON HIS OWN 37

SAINT AUGUSTINE'S TEETH, CANNON XXIX. 38

NAPKINS. 40

HOLY ISLAND 42

Holy Island (One) 42

Holy Island (Two) 42

Holy Island (Three) 43

Holy Island (Four) 44

Holy Island. (Five) 44

Holy Island. (Six) 45

Holy Island (Seven) 45

Holy Island (Eight) 46

Holy Island. (Nine) 47

Holy Island (Ten) 47

Holy Island (Eleven) 48

Holy Island (Twelve) 49

Holy Island (Thirteen) 50

Holy Island. (Fourteen) 51

Holy Island (Fifteen) 51

Holy Island (Sixteen) 52

Holy Island (Seventeen) 55

On Holy Island. 56

Notes on Holy Island. 56

WHEN THE DARKNESS, STIRS… 58

ST CUTHBERT AND THE SEAL. 59

HARRY 60

SONG: WE KNOW YOU'LL COME AND FIND US 61

THE ROOT AND THE BRANCH 62

WHISKY PRIEST TO HIS PEOPLE. 63

THE STEPS 65

NOTES ON STEPS 97

THE UNIVERSE UNFOLDS AS IT SHOULD 99

FRIETH PARISH CHURCH 100

NOTES 101

On writing religious poetry: A brief essay. 101

THE TALE OF THE CHRISTMAS RABBIT. 104

Requiem for a boy chorister.

Seldom has this cathedral seemed small
-it's so unplanned, this harrowing grief-
how happy it was with its' quiverfull.
Too cold, too cold, for those who seek relief.

Gargoyles and statues
scarce help uplifted eyes:
St Peter seems so uncertain.
Crumbling is no way to feed a flock.

Music, young and pure whilst ancient
seems to shallow all flesh, all that grief.
Voices wholly for two mothers' sons, sing,
proclaiming them in the tradition, old boys.

1987.

The first stanza was re-written in 1999.

Seldom has this cathedral seemed small,
in its enormity,   scarce contains such grief,
how happy it was with its' quiverfull,
its ancient cold, numbs those who seek relief.

Liberation

It is a fearful thing to fall into the hands of the living God

Hebrews, 10.31

"Three day s public mourning for Brazilian Archbishop

whom the Pope kissed, despite helping found "Liberation"

dissident theology". (The _____ August 1999)

There is a man who believes he is God
who has been locked away, for safety
he tried to leap of buildings, thinking
he could fly,. He couldn't, he kept breaking things.

There is a man who used to have a pen pal God
he locked his letters away, for safety;
he tried to keep form building, thinking
thoughts of why?. He couldn't. He kept speaking things.

There is a man who talks to God
when he is locked away; in safety
within the keep of buildings, thinking.
He would try, but couldn't, he kept hearing things.

There is a man who listens to God
when his hearts unlocked, risking safety
for a tide in his thoughts is building, thinking,
you must fly. He couldn't, he kept breaking things.

For the man who listened to God
found justice locked, forsake safety
and began the work of building, thinking,
asking, Why?. He couldn't, without breaking things.

*There's a man who believes in God
who has been locked away for safety
whose leap of faith is building, thinking
we could fly. He couldn't, but we are breaking things.*

Huddersfield. 1999

Evensong, York Minster

"My soul doth magnify the lord
and my spirit has rejoiced in God my Saviour
for he that is mighty hath magnified me.
For he hath regarded the lowliness of his handmaiden
for behold, all generations shall call me blessed."

Voices, pure and ancient
Ascend ancient arches
to the words of the Magnificat
and the boy aged five, who has never
heard such sounds,
it echoes in his soul
and he is lost in wonder.

Give me the boy until he is five
and I will give you the man.

Voices, pure and ancient
ascend those same ancient arches
to the words of the Magnificat
and the woman, his fiancé, who has never
heard such sounds
it echoes around her soul
and she is lost in wonder.

Give me the boy until he is five
and I will give you the man.

Voices, pure and ancient,
have yet to be revealed
in the words of the Magnificat
to their boy, to young yet to have ever
heard such sounds
and quite possibly he won't choose,
and yet, may perhaps, wonder.

The Soul of the Preacher

*In the soft white sheen of sandstone
the Bishop lies in eternal peace
with his hands clasped in the blessing
he proclaimed daily to atone*

*for the sins of vanity, whose name
is the garments, so well captured
by the mason, and in the blessing
that lead them to inscribe the stone*

"The Lord is Mighty and Greatly to be Feared".

*The mason was a Latin illiterate
but the priest supplied the text
understood that fear, fear,
fear etched in ignorance is unworthy.*

*So he with white hair and soft eyes
clasped those rough hands and
urged that a dove lie above them
with the moon and the stars below.*

*Fear he said is the firmament,
and so long as there is night,
so long as there is day
there will be a season to the times of
men and a dove to fly above them.*

*The Lord is Mighty and Greatly to be feared.
And the mason replied, let the dove
hide in the tall grass, amongst
the lilies of the field*

*And let the moon and the stars
rest in their accustomed place
that men may look on them and wonder
and the priest smiled his stony smile
and walked away, he quickened his pace
he redoubled his pace
he stopped and turned, and he ran*

*to the sanctuary and clasped his hands
and prayed silently,
"may the peace of the Lord be always with you"
and watching him, the mason replied
"and also with you."*

*The dove never escaped the grass,
and the moon outshines the sun
and the priest enclosed the tomb
with a screen of sandstone
to ensure eternal peace
and that hands clasp in blessing
and that in the living proclaim*

*"The Lord is Mighty and Greatly to be Feared"
and the echo sounds within that empty chamber,*

Thy will be done.

1999

The Blue Bell

*The patterner relaxed
and thought of spring
and when creation was
young.*

*He sketched a flower
and framed canvas
in a beech wood frame*

*and hung it above his
drawing board,*

*He was chalking up
the Chilterns
at the time.*

*From then on,
The hills sort of flowed.*

Freith. 2000

"Dorian" Toccata and Fugue in D Minor BVW 538

1

Softly spoken, in antiphon/
it was old fashioned/
to be not quite whispered/
for the theme was gentle/
and yet the pedal firm/
and with flowing lilt/.

2

The Dorian is the art of arpeggio;
more than melody, it is rise and fall
the moment between life and death and all
where the story of both is clearly told:
Just a latticed garden gate, through which we go.

For a while, there are pictures in the granite,
the colours in the window, sharp then blurred,
The mind wandering in mellowed, subterfuged,
sharp surprise un-rolls.
You realise that the fugue is actually finite.

3

For fear of dreaming
on long journeys
I never take the tape.

Even though I love it so,
at the end of it,
am I am never quite awake.

It is better, still, in church,
If your eyes are shut
people think you praying

Sometimes, just so.

Beautus qui intellegit.

*Blessed is he that considereth the poor and needy
The Lord shall deliver him in the time of his trouble.
Psalm 41.*

*He looked in need of delivery,
he was a subway hood, atop bin bag
with mongrel to accompany his boots.*

*"Beatus qui intellegit" he said to me.
"May the saints in heaven preserve us,
Jesus and Mary wept", thought I.*

*The subways in his eyes, upon me,
the twinkle, as he judged me thinking
what price, delivery?*

*50p for a cup of tea, sir? The missions
open in half an hour sir.*

*I paid the asking price, twice,
and walked away,
the big issue being,
when did we give beggars
the gift of tongues?*

*His delivery was faultless
and it is an uncommon Latin tag,
He called after me and said,
"The evenings drag, don't they sir!*

*I felt a shade unreal at that,
and then, it occurred to me,
" Beautus qui intellegit" is
both a duty and a law:
Angels don't keep dirty dogs.*

I was Glad

Part One

"Jerusalem is builded as city
that is at unity
with itself.

O pray for the peace of Jerusalem
They shall prosper that love thee."

Psalm CXXII

We baptise this Child
In the name of the father
the son, and the Holy Ghost.

The Romans began this place
and the Saxons added on,
the Normans built a tower
and the Victorians, well
never mind that aisle,
the lighting is quite modern
and the music is well sung.

It is a variety of arches
I sketched whilst a boy
to demonstrate that
I could fly a buttress
while mastering the simple
rise and fall of
Norman grace.

In quires and place where they sing,
here followeth the anthem.
"I was glad", by Parry, I was
I chose it. As I said, well sung.

They thought it wise to stress the unity,
although she took the place by storm,
as I knew she would: She is highly polished
A Cannon, well placed, and slightly surrounded
and eminently placed to proclaim admittance
to our mother church.

I chose the Cannon wisely
being one of the first
of the women to bless that office
in my less than early Church.

There are some that may that might find it odd
that I who choose to process with Cramner
should embrace the women's priestly stole
whole heartedly. Indeed, it is odd, but as I said

The Romans began this place and there is something
to be said for buttressing our faith with modern
arches. And, remembering that Romans began this place;
it is by returning to our beginnings that we can trace our faith.

Part Two

"For my brethrens and companions sakes,
I will wish thee prosperity".

Down at the Seaman's Mission
she was a Deaconess
and as she was also my
Great Aunt,
I recall her tenderness.

She died when I was young
but her "farthing fund" provided
for excursions to the seaside
and other amusements.
As I say, when I was young.

Part Three

I have those farthings hoarded,
my share, at least, well guarded,
I keep them safe but show them

sometimes to my children
when they ask me of who
it is provides for them

days out at the sea side
and other amusements.
They too are young.

Part Four

"They that go down to the sea in ships
these men see the works of the Lord
and his wonders in the deep" (Psalm CVII)

Are the waters calmer now
than they were in Galilee
when a stranger called on
two fishermen? I doubt it.

And it still the case that
the tide turns twice a day
in Galilee? And that in between,
in the hope of catching more
the fishermen mend their nets?

And the questions still remain.
Would we rather our children sing
"with bread and fishes and a
cup of red wine" than sit and watch
us as we mend out nets?

And if your arms are folded,
Believing that I am wrong,
I pray that you will forgive me.

*If you will fish with me in Galilee
we can feel the tidal race
and hope that wind beats surely
on those seeking haven, with God's Grace.*

The Cathedral

1 The Regimental Chapel

Regimental flags hang still
there is no history here of wind
only the faintest breath of breeze
as a door is opened or perhaps, shut.

The Battalion sits for church parade
pews as ram-rod as backs well drilled.
There is no need to right dress here,
men rest easy. A minor cannon, surpliced

receives their colours, faded and thin
bright in sunshine, then perpetually dim.
The honours are sounded, the fanfare salutes;
an old breath of life bids tattered comrades in truth.

2 The Path above Arches

High above arches, a walkway is hidden
with stairs to the tower that go up to the top
crews use it now days for cameras and shots
'murder in the cathedral'; TV's cathedra pops.

I wondered as a child, how you could go?
Who gave permission? Who would know?
It was the verger who took me, a kindly old man,
before the privation, nowadays, only camera men can...

3 The Aisles

Taverner's anthem, the one we all know,
- the music we all cried to, as Diana' coffin slow marched,
from dais to the door, on shoulders well borne -
I hear from the choir stalls, hidden from sight.

This is that theatre where you see not the stage
when sitting in stalls, the priesthood talks far away
until they bid you stand up, walk down the straight aisle
breathless, you receive communion, kneeling, a child.

Today is choir practise, and I walk a sad while
up to the Lady Chapel, light a candle, revile
a tourist who chatters to that lament of a prayer
look at the Colours, breath in deep and fresh air.

At her wedding she chose, vowing to thee, her country.
This place is huge, sound echoes, most tall and so ordered.
Light plays on the flowers - just like the strewn -
arranged always on Saturdays by the Mothers' Union rule.

4 The Ventilation

We read our musty service books
The boys still sing in starchy ruffs
The incense burns like sickly sweets
Air conditioning would soon defeat
our memories, them 'summoned by smells'!

Were I to tell a tale of old Sir John
I would choose by nose, a copy, woe begone!
Were I to tell a tale of old Sir John?

5 The Porch

There is a notice by the door
bids you pray if you go in at all.
It is odd that there's a paper to remind
people to remember how to pay in kind.

6 The Lady Chapel

I could not travel that saddest day
family reasons kept me far away
as they laid to rest, the gentlest
of women with whom a child was blessed.

On that day my parish would not do at all
I drove to Wakefield, sat in a borrowed stall
said a silent service, singing inward hymns.
The setting was my sorrow. I brought sadness in
the nave was big enough to take it,

forever sound, forever solid.
I don't know just how long I sat there,
but the verger minded, bid me take care.

7 The Porch (ii)

The 'poor box' is as ancient, battered as the roof
its venerable dents, encourage the reproof...
when lightning struck a second hole appeared;
they labeled one 'mission', the other, 'buildings in fear...'

8 The Screen

An axe falls and with it a tree
a century cleaved is a millennium born
a sharp grained stroke of certainty.

Who wielded the axe? No one knows, but
his hands were marked, his flesh was torn.
The beam is a straight as a falling blow.

9 The Bishops Chapel

The Bishop died in fourteen ninety three
all else I guess, it's a Latin eulogy,
or rather, I don't as time has moved on
I rely on the guidebook, they translated his sea…".

10 The Quad

My old mate Cuthbert
squelched the self-same dirt.
However much I follow
He's way ahead of me.

My old mate Cuthbert
sheltered in this quad.
Would marvel at the spoken
the broken word of God.

My old mate Cuthbert
settled by the sea
cathedrals were too busy
harboured not the launch of

this weathered city, this rain.

11 The Psalter in the Pew

Abide with me
we bid the departing tide.
With the poetry of psalms
and David's kindred son we mind.

12 The Vestry

A robing dean dons a singsong voice
flowing and flaxen, he rumbles a klaxon
weaving consonants softy and rolling his 'rrrr's
his vowels are as velvet as the coated cut of cloth.

Only these days they don't! They pick baleful cotton
embellish pale chequered suits, with this years' buttons.
The fiore has softened to that flame-thrilled accent
that makes hell fire simmer to a barbecue's descant.

They adorn a 'maison', the Deanery being sold
put the hospital in hospitaller, with charity bold
the hardships of Harding, all those drafts and big fires
so much better that the Close has been profitably acquired.

Give me a Dean, a rumbusteous Dean,
cranking and creaking, proverbially spleen
with coffers, the toffers and the doffers, you see?
A Dean is an occasion, should be too big to demean.

13 The Baptistery

In Times-old-Roman, they christened the font.
However they edit, or re-order the rest
the Font stands unchanged, in three pointed text.

14 The Treasury

Today is the day for scouts
they forage and search, reconnoiter the church
scampering here, hiding there.
The scouts are quite lively, high pitched and

The Bishop is here for the scouts!
He talks of tents and lights the campfire!
Jesus is calling; he's a real live wire!
The Bishop is lively, high pitched and he sounds
as if he's un-knotted the mysteries

with which young-life abounds

The Cathedral has captured some scouts!

15 The Choir Stalls

A boy of seven enters all timidly
even smaller than small, in somewhere so tall.
There is so much silence but no assembly here.
Where is the head, to tell all to be quiet?

Sound of boys singing, but not nursery rhymes,
long soft notes that sound almost round.
They dress so funny, are no older than he.

With the wide eyes of a child, he asks:
'How can I meet, the small,
the angel-call-singing man?'

16 The Choir Stalls (ii)

The Cathedral preserves
Evensong and serves
to prevent spreading jam
smothering Crammer's lamb.
The teashop serves cream, and tea.

17 The Vergers Pew

Glass stained light plays with the curves in stone
hues and shadows shaped in the lead lined eve,
whose breath dapples lowly summer's rustling leaves.

Ever onwards towards the screen, that wood
which kept the distance well between and stood
to soften the shadows, setting softly sun ripened eaves.

The gargoyles stare blindly as the lively swing and sway,
smiling kindly in the certainty that struck ugliness away.
The handmade features fashioned for generations blessed.

The colours flash on our new model army as they tilt
this way and that, perpendicular to the mystery and doubt.
The reds in the George window seem almost to shout

where is the history? Whose lance do they bear?
Through the ages soft tempers worded people here -
The cavaliers and roundheads un-hatted at the door.

The light in shafts falls next on the pulpit, on the bible
whose leaf pages sparkle gold, God's world is at play;
for a butterfly moment a moth is lit more than grey.

The verger watches quietly, he knows this mood.
Looks at the flags for which so much blood was spilt;
A boy asks him which king was it built? He stoops, 'Well..

Notes on 'The Cathedral'.

The Cathedral is not modeled on one particular cathedral but is a reflection on Cathedrals I have visited. It is of course a reflection on the past, present and future use of cathedrals and their place within the evolution of the Anglican Communion.

Thanks to The Rev Mark Janes who once again helped sort the wheat from the chaff. DJA.

vii: revised October 2014.

Confutatis Requiem

Death was creeping down the aisle
full in the face of God,
the priest, he beamed encouragement;
I must have looked a frightened child.

Damning the tradition
I turned and faced her.

the sweet tranquility of her face
raises in me a doubt;
can it be that I have feared
one whose eyes adore,
and why do I condemn
those quiet, perfect lips?
And why try to distance
one whose form so gratifies?
Did ever such grace delight?
Was ever a virgin so pure?

That moment was its' doubt,
The colonnades and arches, temples and churches
crashed down.
Headless and with all my blood displayed,
death will be my bride
though sodden, in white arrayed
and yes by the Grace of God.

Huddersfield, 1987.

Confutatis Requiem Revisited : Grief undeserved.

As this dread hour I face,
who will tell my story,
be it sound, be it fury
will it amount to grace?

Years ago, damning tradition
I turned and faced her,

lured into bed with Mozart
sepulchral refrain and anthem
I embraced abs-, resolution.

Death to the traitor!
Love conquers Death!
Love conquers all?

Down trodden, dismayed
-though sodden, in white arrayed-
I am the despisers' toy,
un-wrapped, un-made
my grief, the game he plays.

2

Am I quieter now?
I burn inside, but softly.
Can you tell? I am passion
I am anger, I am torment,
I am the fuse still lit.

Am I quieter now?
I yearn inside, but softly.
I can tell all? Without passion,

the stranger, the tormenter,
the tortured, lip split.

In a room, quite room
It is never day, nor night.
How shall I know me?
All is shadows, nothing light.
Am I dead, or living fright?

The situations grave, there is
no marvel, no one to embrace.
No one opens the door, is there
a door? They have taken my face?
There is nothing, nothing in its place!

Am I quieter now?
I fade inside, but softly
I have lost all, am outwith passion.
The man, the boy, lover, father
I deny, denied all of it. I am, am not.

3

The cock crows, thrice,
the strangled laughter, diced,
it's for the mincer made,
with all its blood displayed

There is no room for doubt
only the witless flout
their broken toys, a child's love
lost to the anger of angels above.

Take up your cross, my cherubs!
or damn you, despite's cubs!

In breaking him, you crucified me.
Spare him. Spare me, be ungodly;

It was not yours to take, this life
it was yours to make, blessing thrice.
Who are you, angels of God to curse
the additions, perfect cognito, divide the sum.

"Prove all things, hold fast to that which is good"

(Thessalonians, 5.21)

In a room, more empty than full
the man puts on his robes
and smiles as I, his acolyte, enter to
light the wick and thereafter the candles.

He says the service quickly, and his sermon is as short
as his monks close cropped hair; he gets to the point,
rebuts it sadly and leaves a melancholy air.
He knew we boys wanted out of there.

They say he died of, he died of an overburdened heart
for you can shake the man but it is hard to fell the priest.
He was of a band of pilgrims, disbanded,
and in a parish found it hard to progress at all.

And yet, he let me light the candles
and would say to me
"to do so is to acquire merit"
which at the time did not strike me
odd.

Not that he was a Buddhist; he had a Christian soul,
merely that he was a teacher without rebuttal
but in me, for no then apparent reason
he lit the wick, and thereafter the candles
of faith, of that still small voice
that allows for a reasonable doubt
and which arguably, leaves room for merit.

When I struggle, and when I am not long on faith
I run a hand through close-cropped hair
just like a statue I know, called "the Thinker".
That he would reasonably assert, is to easy
but then he also let me blow the candles out.
I missed the point of course, he didn't.
Our time was sadly short.

*With deepest respect for
and with affection,
for a Father of a former Anglican
Religious Order.*

1999.

Every man 'neath his vine and fig tree.

A dove flew into a willow tree,
Will you weep, weep for me?
The tree remained silently
Ignorant of the petitioners' plea.

The dove returned to its cot
Hardly peaceful when such
A number make quite a lot
Of noise that means not much.

The tree has empty branches
Ready to rake un-swept ground
When the wind howls at the haunches
Of preening, perched, muted crowds.

A delectable, deafening sound.

One scratch, one peck, one head.

2003

Catch a devil on his own

and look him in the eye
and he will sell you
toothpaste or insurance
or perhaps a hoover bag.

All he has to do is wait
for the followers of fashion
to enter his mall, arcade,
searching for a bargain
or perhaps, just an
indulgence or lampshade.

Angels never sell you
anything,
only the devil has
anything to trade.

The devil is a
store detective.
Eventually you'll pay.

(2001)

Saint Augustine's teeth, Cannon XXIX.

Deep routed in the vine
that strangles the unwary
he remained in his seat
for though the blood
of saints flows within
his veins, the cup and
the body of Christ
is by cannon law,
denied him.

The bishop in the palace,
the poor man at his gate
the sheep that safely graze
and the excluded, the goat,
have their place.

He chews on the offered blessing
and for six months remains in his place
as the faithful file on past him
and he grinds his teeth, sharpening
to ensure that in atonement
he will be able to swallow the
words of the prayer book
without chewing them
even once.

Even Christ spent only forty days,
he spent six months,
and don't you know, my faithful reader,
he atoned for the sins of the father
he atoned for the sins of the son
and he atoned for the whispering sands

and he atoned in silence, but in his heart
he stored up these things up in his heart.

Saint Augustine's teeth need polishing
and are perhaps not quite as bright
as a modern image requires,
for with gaping gaps in its smile
the unwary have their faith devoured.

Saint Augustine's teeth need pulling
for they offend those that suffer
with the aches and pains of pilgrimage
and for those less strangled by the vine
than he has been from birth,
the wilderness might have been, too much.

Should ever the cannons roar again,
he has promised to take battle
right to the Bishop's door
and with Cannon Thirty
fire incense whilst drinking
goats milk in a silver cup.

Huddersfield. 2000

Napkins.

I am not sure that I know
If indeed tomorrow it will snow
Sure enough it is certain cold
But not enough to unfold

A napkin or tablecloth
Over all the hillocks
Or say that nature
Must be for sure

Predicted.

That does not stop them
Oiling the toboggan
It must slip and it must slide
Never mind and woe betide

The afflicted.

Time was and time was
When I enjoyed
Fluffy stars that sparkled bright.
All around, enchanted night.

So Excited.

Now I wonder if in fact
I will reach the shop all-right
Its not that I am curmudgeonly
Just afraid, aged, snowed and sluggardly.

Spring will mend the broken blades
They will green and stand again
I know only that which I recall
Nothing must follow anything at all.

I will fold the napkins
Iron the tablecloth
Leave open the curtains
And when I sit down, say grace.

HOLY ISLAND

Holy Island (One)

Fifth gear to open the road
as I speed like a north easterly
gale, a driving force of turbulence, and accelerating,
I am the cyclone that tears up the road,
the storm surge, that sweeps all in its path,
I am the tempest, I am
all blown out, exhausted.
I am the flotsam, blowing north easterly,
on the ebb of the tide, that will land on a beach
beneath a small country hotel
with real beams, driftwood arches,
and an open log fire
that smokes through a chimney
depositing ash, on the windscreen
of a car that must be cleaned,
before reclaiming the road.

Holy Island (Two)

The boy sits at the kitchen table,
he is chewing on the offered sweet,
considering if a trip to an island is a treat,
his five year old brow is furrowed,
as Mummy is not coming too.
His parents suspect cold feet,
in swift reverse suggest he is not old enough
"I am so"! I ask him if he is taller than
the door of the freezer as only big boys..
He grabs a printer label and says "what
number must I be?" "120": he writes it
and with his back to the frigidaire
he pastes the label to the door and
then turns triumphantly to say "there"
I am tall enough" Laughing, I tell him
that Mummy will help select his gear.

Holy Island (Three)

It is neither Aiden, nor Cuthbert I seek,
still less the ruins of faith that call
but the living company of pilgrims
who continue to gather, after the fall
of communities of the set apart....
What I wonder did Aiden and Cuthbert seek?
The living call of the pilgrim, and a gathering.
Is that what I seek? Resurrection and the Life?
All that I really know for sure, is that
the tide will rise, closing the mainland road.
I am of an Island race, is it strange therefore,
that we retreat into a shoreline we can walk?
Pil-grim? An austere
benediction, this path I follow?
In stating my denial,
I find questions that keep
arising about that
Aiden and Cuthbert.
It is true of course, I could read a book, but then,
a living history, requires that you take in the view.
In Yorkshire we call that, the 'nook'.

Holy Island (Four)

A fork in the road
renders York
to the traveller.
Being hungry,
I make a voluntary
donation to
Macdonalds
and am
poorly fed,
yet, The boy
adores the plastic
cartoon dog.
He, the coeliac,
has a burger
without the bread...

Holy Island. (Five)

How tall is the Minster?
Was he glad? He was curious
which at five, is a beginning
and in feet I estimated the gates.
Unconscious of his baptism
he headed straight for the candles
which stand opposite. At the
turn of the hour, in earshot of
the celestial clock. He is struck
silent, mesmerised. He turns to me
and puts a face on it: "What time is it?"
He knows not his hours, neither his minutes,
and yet, for a moment it seems important
to know the what, the why, the wherefore,
that only a father can impart. I answer him.
Having not told him that it is his time, I ask him
to turn his face to the Great Rose Window
he marvels at the colours which he wants to draw
and I explain that which they have been for and age and more.

There is no music, the Choir is on holiday, as are we,
on checking the time of evensong, remember that
the 10th of August is indeed St Lawrence's Day.
I tell the story of a deacon, a teacher, and he
becomes all shy and bashful, as a lay clerk
tells me that today a communion will be said.
He wanders off, to examine a statue, and
turns to me and says " Did the clock strike, Daddy
when they were alive", I have stored up enough
to kneel before our exit, and offer a minute's thanks.
He stamps his foot, 'what next' he asks.

Holy Island. (Six)

Is it in the path of the Venerable Bede,
or in search of the Lindisfarne Mead
that I have gone in retreat?
It is the Mead from the Gift Shop
that I unpack first of all;
other gifts take more unwrapping.

Holy Island (Seven)

On taking a trip from Seahouses
we visit a gathering of seals,
I cannot recall having seen
so many together.
He, never having seen a seal before,
simply does not bother to count.
For him, it is joy without numbers.
For me, it is roll of film that runs
out halfway, and has to be changed.
Over breakfast next morning
it is his account the strangers
in our B + B, listen too. Not Me.
No one wants to hear that I saw
a puffin, for the first time.
I cannot convey the moment of a
first discovery, and it was too quick
to catch a photo to create
the opportunity

to bore my wife and friends.
My story must remain untold,
and I thought this retreat was about
me discovering me.
The boy borrowed my camera
only once, so there is only one
photo of, anyone but he.

Holy Island (Eight)

Bamburgh Castle stands high and tall
with Norman arches and panelled hall,
with cannon, and gated portcullis,
a family home, a fine estate.
It is the skyline, is the tradition
of arches and ascendance contained.

The Castle of Lindisfarne,
a movement of monumental
force, against the outcrop
of resurgent natural stone.
A reminder that man has not lived
relying on the auspice of faith alone.

The Lights' of the Farne Isles
have gathered the sailors home
and have guided from the rocks
almost all, but some were lost
despite the best efforts of those
who dwelt alone behind iconic locks.

Wherever we draw the line
between coast and sea
between earth and sky
there is a roughness at the edges
and a rude refusal of rock to
sit quietly, and weather the ages
idly by. Not even the mason
can halt this sure and certain truth:
Despite the best endeavour of men
it is only the eye that ever rests.

Holy Island. (Nine)

Within a rock pool
we discover a hermit crab.
I am the pupil, moulded to the shape
of a master who knows not what to teach.
It is enough, merely to be, to grab with a pincer
at whatever experience I may direct to pass by.
He being not strong enough I lift the rocks
to see what discoveries lie underneath.
We marvel at a tiny starfish, and he collects
shells to show his teacher, when they are washed.
Then it is time to go in for dinner, and I negotiate food
without wheat, rye, barley or oats, it being only months
since he would not eat, save water, his fear stunting growth.
The hotelier offers soup. I am stroppy, and rice, boiled with cheese
is delivered, at a made up price, on speaking to a manager
who instructs the cook who was too busy, to take the risk
of taking the bread out of the mouths of children .
On returning to my room, I reach for the mead, but
replace the bottle; it is his bed time. I read
him a story. With tummy ache he pleads
that I will ensure that he has milk, and that
I will remember at breakfast, he cannot eat much.
I gaze at the shells, and wish I had claws.

Holy Island (Ten)

The Priory lies smashed
by weather, and by men.
A testament to forces that
once unleashed, cared nothing
for the purposes of builders.

The preservation is well done,
and the museum is well run.
The chapel is still standing
and continues what was begun.

The design is simple, and only
core fragments of stone remain..
Simple words were said in this place.

Simple words, where now, in a field
adjoining, once again, and to quote

"sheep may safely graze".
In dissolution, and with time,
they achieved,
Openness and mystery. In woe, they begun.

Holy Island (Eleven)

Lest there be injustice,
to an excellent B +B
they acquired cornflakes
and served what he
could and would eat.
Whilst full, they were not
too busy to accommodate me.
I have penned a letter to someone
who can award a crown.
And if you will pardon the verse,
it befits that they be so hatted
and not hated,
And if you will forgive the verse
they fried eggs, toasted bread
into soldiers, and being good folk
so ensured he ate the yolk.
I hoped to leave my anger behind
on that ancient and blessed island.
Don't you know, my faithful reader,
Perhaps if I return next year,
I will not have to constantly explain.
That would be nice, for, I would not
wish to teach him that to succeed in
even little things
you need complain.
In my excellent B +B
they acquired cornflakes
and will perhaps again,
accommodate me.
Having paid in cash,
and issued a credit note,
and sent a thank you card,

*I feel that with this verse
I have almost but not quite
settled the bill.
Almost, as unlike them,
I could have done this better
but other meals elsewhere
have clouded my skill.*

Holy Island (Twelve)

On staring out over a summers evening sea,
I recall a Celtic blessing,
*"Deep peace of the running wave be with you,
Deep peace of the moon and stars be with you."*
Only, in the calm of the evening,
the waves are still,
and the full moon lies low
in an otherwise orange sky.
I am Ethelred,
challenging the waves
to stop. I am unready,
I turn my back on the evening
and, reflect that the light is on
the rook pools are that peculiar hue
which captures the moment before
day becomes night. And, try as I might
I retreat into myself, piece by piece,
I know that has this not been the day
when I will allow care to wash away.
I am still scribbling out the message
that I have been bottling up.
As the light fades,
I return to bed,
too tired to write
or read.
There is sheen across the bay
as the moon asserts its place
and the stars, gently mingle
in a dance, that runs away.
And as they play,
I will the waves
to join the fray

*and carry far
and carry long
a bottle, I hurl
into the bay.
It occurs to me
that I found
from somewhere
the only two lines
that I had
the strength to pray.*

Holy Island (Thirteen)

*I wonder why it is
that what he wanted
most from the gift shop
was a camera that is his.
His old one he had buried
and it is no longer alive
as it is in back garden lawn
and I should have known!
He has a proper paddy
when I find not one
and is not comforted by
the offer of sharing mine;
No longer mine but,.
This is his first holiday
away with me, alone
and as he drags me to
the next shop, I wonder
if I had realised that
he has now discovered
that he has memories
he wants to call his own.
And he pulls me bodily in
and out of shops that might
provide the means of showing
his friends and teachers
his story of his treat.
What I really am wondering
is where I was when he
discovered that he was*

quite so colourfully developed.
That look in his eyes as he
stomps me towards the counter
is so clearly focussed, that I
feel that he has been playing
with the daylight,
whilst I have been in a dark
a dark room, under-exposed, and
am emerging blinded by
an image of myself
when I was convinced
that I was quite simply
right. Perhaps by candle light?
I buy the camera;
if he can choose his moments
perhaps with the aid of an album
I stand just an outside chance of
staying in the race.
Or at least
Looking him in the face?

Holy Island. (Fourteen)

On seeing the sunset
he remarks that
the sun has leaked
all over the sky.

Holy Island (Fifteen)

"All we like sheep,
have gone astray"
Off the beaten track it does not
do to wander for the signs warn
of quick sand that will
swallow the unwary.
I drove across the causeway
and did not walk the ancient,
less than safe -in fact,
downright risky- pilgrims way.
Have I made all of this too easy?

*Or is it even possible that
my mission here has been only,
Merely,*

*nearly, to be the observer of
another who seems surer
as he assembles material
for his own, and as of yet
unfocussed and uncharted
quest?
It is equally possible that
the answers I seek,
are simply not here.*

I cannot expect him to be clear.

Holy Island (Sixteen)

"Blessed is He who comes in the name of the Lord.
Hosanna in the highest." The Benedictus.

"Our soul is escaped even as a bird out of the snare of the fowler:the snare is broken, and we are delivered." Psalm 124

*Down at the harbour,
he asked me to
explain a lobster pot.
The material point
is that the Lobster cannot
escape un-aided.
Just to underline the point
he asks me,
"isn't is scary
if they are still alive"
I believe that Lobsters
as they grow are
also required
to shed their skin.
Yes, Lobsters are scary monsters
and terribly thick skinned
Sea-Food for thought.*

***
I wonder vaguely
if I will be a trifle
or just a wafer thin mint
when it comes to thinking
about what it is will be
for desert. Silly Me.

***

We walk back towards our
guest house,
examining the hulk of what
was once a working
fishing boat.
There was a time upon
reaching this harbour
the mate would throw
a line, which would be
caught and tied.
It occurs to me,
that in some strange way
despite my best endeavours
attempts have been made
to throw me a line.
In fact as I sit on this bench
I am wondering quite which
part of creation, was not
quite so deliberately
meant.
***
Behind the Priory
is lit a brilliant sky
in fact,
is quite the
"benedictus"
the builder
intended.
"Blesssed is he
who comes in
the name of

*the Lord."
and by my side
a little boy
is sketching
It is nearly bedtime
and I tell him to
gather up his things
as it is time to go.
He asks me
to carry his picture safely,
He has drawn a fisherman
gathering lobster pots,
on a sea that is blue
and beneath a sky
that is gold.
I promise him hot chocolate
as a treat,
before I tuck him into bed.
He asks me if he can unlock the
door to our room as we enter
our B+B.
He is learning how to turn a key.
We decide that tomorrow
we will be up early.
He wants to walk the beach
before we break our fast.*

***

*I recall - in the words of Saint
Chrysostom,- this, my second
prayer:
"Where two or three are gathered together
in thy Name, thou wilt grant their requests,
Fulfil, now, O Lord, the desires and petitions
of thy servants, as may be most expedient
to them. Granting in this world knowledge
of thy truth, and in the world to come,
life everlasting."
And that night
it really seemed
that not two but
three,*

*had gathered there.
After hot chocolate,
I was granted
sound and deep sleep.
deep peace of moon and star
deep and dreamless sleep
such as once I knew.*

Holy Island (Seventeen)

*People imagine
the remnants of prayer;
that saintly spirits keep
their daily office in
perpetual echo of that
holiness which pervades
this aptly named Isle.
We forget
that Holiness is a challenge
that makes no excuses
and that it is not the
echo's of service past
but the promises
of tomorrow renewed
that sanctify this isle.
I was blown here
on avenging wing
angry and
without care or prayer.
I leave this place
more of a father
and more of son
and more knowing
of the work to be done.
And what of Aiden and Cuthbert?
Are they smiling somewhere?
I came seeking a quick and
easy fix. That is not, and
never has been the rule.
First discharge your obligations
to the world, for it is not*

enough to be set apart;
you must be released.
Smile, my Saints smile,
I very nearly failed
to understand the test.
But not quite.
It has been in daily life
that I have been cut off
and it is there I must more
carefully, learn,
where to place my feet.
No man is an island
save he choose to be.
And that is not an option
when your calling is family.
It is a long drive home.

On Holy Island.

The visit to Holy Island described was the "Millennium Project" that I decided to undertake. Holy Island has held my curiosity since I started some ten years ago or more, flying past it heading to or from Edinburgh on the East Coast Line.
The poem was largely written over four days, and I acknowledge the able assistance of my brother, the Rev Mark Janes, in editing and revising it. I think The Boy *enjoyed his "treat".DJA,. 2000*

Notes on Holy Island.

It is my habit to subtitle my collections with "poems, we doubt".
Partly, because that reflects both the material I am working with, and the way I treat it.
Holy Island as a work makes significant use of plain speech, does not use a standard form, or have immediately apparent rhyming schemes. However, that freedom in form, allows carefully constructed themes, and connections between sections of the work to be accentuated. It is also apparent that in sections I wanted to think aloud with my reader; plain speech is in my view an appropriate device to achieve this end that the teaching of poetry often explores with less merit than this device deserves.

Doubt is an essential engine of faith. In fact, it can be surprising where it can take you. It also allows for wonderful moments of certainty, which benefit from the processes of both deduction and revelation

Coeliacs disease is a condition that makes a person intolerant of anything containing glutens: and a reasonable proportion of our diet contains the cereals and their derivatives that can have serious consequences for the coeliac. Ronald Macdonald would make me very happy by providing gluten free meals worldwide; others might follow?

Incidentally, Canute got wet, Ethelred was unready. Poetic licence almost extends to re-writing history, but not quite?

DJA 2000

When the darkness, Stirs...

Soft, softly, quiet, quietly, smoothly
He plucks the nylon stings,
A candle flickers, some burning oil
A velvet cushion on the floor
Perhaps whispers, perhaps purrs.
He is salt on my tongue
He is my wakefulness
He is bitter but sweet
Not the singer for the song.
All around me the young
Wonder how to waltz
Wonder who Matilda
Yawn a jolly swag man
Did they beat the drum slowly?
It is the song before bed time
Generations of calm, calming
Sleep softly, young Willy McBride.

St Cuthbert and the Seal.

Cuthbert sitting on a rock
was visited by a seal
who gave him quite a shock
by sharing in his meal.

The saint sat rather still
thinking a hermits real
company is God's will
blessed the thief; the seal.

Knocked of that lonely rock.
Cuthbert floundered in the sea
half drowned by his one flock
repents rash charity.

The saint lay rather still
all washed up and beached,
he watched the seal until
beyond his voices reach.

He cursed it all the same,
and then hung his head
feeling in his heart his shame:
blessing the rock, touching, his foes bed.

Basking all, upon a rock
a lonely rock, a well swept rock,
many seals, where no man dare,
to prove that God's chosen
may live alone, un-mocked.

Before the shame of saints'
seas reel.

Harry

Sir Harry Secombe died today.
Goon away.

Sir Harry Secombe died today
We will miss the loud
The tenor of his way.

Sir Harry Secombe died today.
Holy week mourning underway,
imagine Easter sunrise, in his eyes.

Sir Harry Secombe died today.
Every valley was exalted,
and every rough place made plain.

His was the highway,
the laughing falsetto
and the glorious raspberry.

He was truly
larger than life.

Holy Week 2001

Song: We know you'll come and find us

We know you'll come and find us.

We are counting our blessings, we know they are many
You gave us each morning, you gave us the day
And if we are lost and are feeling cold and hungry
We know you'll come and find us.
You help us to play.

We are counting our numbers, we know they are many
We learn them each morning, we count them this way
And if we are lost, and are feeling that their scary
We know you'll come and find us
You help us each day.

We are writing our letters, we know they are many
We learn them each morning, we draw them this way
And if we are lost, and are feeling very weary
We know you'll come and find us
You help us each day.

I am counting my blessings; I know that I'm lucky
I come here each morning, I come here each day
And if I am lost, and feeling that I need you
I know you'll come and find me
You help me each day.

(Repeat verse one -Optional)

To the Tune of 'We gather together': traditional American Thanksgiving Day Song.

The Root and the Branch

That September was April with attitude
Rainbows and squalls, confused as a
cap worn backwards;
that baby faced look
with wind you up sneer.
Lethargy and passion in gusts.

Innocence was on my mind
leaves falling as they usually do
colours taking their autumnal hue
only this year cometh the axe
to remove the moment that
after bitterness, brings colour back.

Over the years the weeds I've tended
but still the bough breaks,
still the beam falls.

There was no raven croaking there
no horses turned and ate their mares
the prophetess cried not of March
no, the bulletins came by telephone
cutting, sharp and heavy, sooner

than the frosts that take lesser things,
annuals, bulbs, lesser things enfeebled.

No, this was autumn with attitude
staking its claim before winter
before ever the cap fits
before we had the measure
of the trees, root and branch
devoid of colour

Whisky priest to his people.

When I was younger
men of Yorkshire would curse
the southern softness of
my inbred linguistic purse.
Whilst not perhaps, quite as rude
as Thomas's welsh and ready curse
to me it was still odd to find
my tongue left them hard-nosed.
It was the older ones that minded
their silence marking them offended
building around them dry stone walls
which no soft rain could hope unfold.
Not that charity was denied me,
a drop o' the hard stuff was offered
when I stepped in from the bitter cold
without asking. A common foe, the cold.
I built bridges with bitter tales, they reminisced
of winters before central heating came to kiss
the comfort loving children goodnight, or else
when roads were blocked, before the gritter's grit.

I learned to listen, swallow the proverbial stone
with mouth open, they saw me, nought but a kid.
Learning my place, was to listen to the lore
that my cloth hatted companions must share before
I could earn the label, right enough. Enough of what?
This is my home, this is my land, not enough, be dammed!
And yet, I left home to see the world -enough said-
if I felt like an immigrant, what did I expect?
One accommodation have I made to my adopted home
for yes, say 'aye' with an accent honed to sound
not quite acquired and not quite native.
Just purse my lips, and let the Yorkshire slip.

Feast of Christ the King
Wakefield 2001
(after R.S Thomas, A Priest to his people).

The Steps

(Reflections over seven nights).

First steps tumbling end;
observed or not
the tendency to catch
is not the lesson
to be taught.

That look of susprise
at both the journey and fall
is impossible to recall

The lesson is still learnt
being there after for granted:
Anything is possible

we just get better
at the prophecy
of risks.

ii

Voices cry out in the wilderness
it is play time.

The world has expanded
into play grounds.

No one guarantees
even the rules of the games.

iii

Lord have mercy
on the little
no one else will

and if they will

do they believe

in pity?

Smite my enemies
little-by-little
no one else will

and if they will

do they believe

in pity?

Lord have mercy
on the little
everyone

and if they will

make them and me

less pitiful.

Iv

The school steps grow taller

several flights, to run up
and fly down, escaping

time and the lessons
that await in corridors
or in the slower pace
of those who play
the waiting game.

*Don't run, walk
is the stupidest rule
enoforced by those too old
to remember that only
the free and the lazy
can saunter or just
find time to stop
and chat, and talk.*

v

*Blessed is the name of the Lord
Hosanna in the highest.*

*So, he walked did he, after
stepping off a donkey
within the gates of Jerusalem.*

*He walked to his destiny,
Death.*

But they cheered him.

*They laid palms at his feet,
Hosanna, son of David,
Hosanna in the Highest,
King of Kings, Lord of Lords
For ever and ever, Amen.*

*The jeered him, whipped and
jabbed with thorns.*

*He walked his cross to calvary
or at least until
some brave follower -Simon of Cyrene -
picked up his cross.*

No doubt, this cheered him.

*Cheered him as he approached
the cross roads of life and death.*

*He measured his moments on earth
in the steps he trod.
Wasn't he afraid, why didn't he
simply run away?
He was God.*

*He was his mothers son
as he walked past her.
Something kept him going,
in her eyes the son of...
vi*

*His first procession,
robed up and starched
with hymn book and ruff.*

*Following the cross,
the chorister in front, keeping
step and turning into the stall
in strict time with his neighbour and
ending with a bow.*

*Oh, he sings, just like at
the rehearsal he learnt to.*

*He did not need reminding
to polish his laced up shoes.*

vii

*He sits and stands
where the pencilled marks
are added to the service book*

*to ensure that even the new boys
can follow the rules.*

*The congregation always follows
as no one scribbles in the hints
for the people in the pews.*

viii

*Joshua walked around Jericho
ambled around shouting
playing the trumpet and drums.*

*Joshua won by rambling
on and on loudly!
Joshua went round in circles*

*until his listeners' defences
came crumbling down.
Joshua strolled the battle of Jericho!*

ix

*God is on his holy hill,
even up a high mountain!*

*Prophets always had to climb
up and up, needed it seems
a good head for heights!*

*OK, the fireworks were good,
burning bushes and the like
and the reading mattered
- ten commandements. On Sinai
one even ascended from sight!*

*In times of old, God recruited goats
to herd his sheep, goats travel light.*

x

*What did God give you legs for
my parents used to say,
half way up a "Ben" something
"High" something else.
The point is, until you're grown up
God only gives you little legs!*

*There was always trouble when they walked down,
people praying to golden rams, or just
not wanting to listen to an angry young man
talking about plagues and famine.*

*In fact, hiding in caves was quite common,
as people don't like the law being laid down.*

*Is it any wonder the those prophets were forever
crying "unclean" and "blow you down".*

*I never wanted to be a prophet,
I always wanted God to come down
fearing my legs were too little
and that I would be shouted
down,
if he made me climb up
enough to herd the goats
and his hill side flock abiding.*

*It also worried me no one taught
Abraham that it is rude to go about
throwing rocks. Sticks and stones
break little bones.*

xi

*St Aidens Gate
beneath the fort at Bamburgh
has ancient stone stairs down
to where his quayside stood.*

*That saintly king would take
boat trips to Cuthbert on
Lindisfarne or perhaps
his abbot would row across*

to take a glass of mead with him.

*Or, perhaps to say a service
or report on the new buildings
and the work of scribing.*

*A set of stairs from sea to cliffe top,
just long enough to collect your thoughts
if you've an audience with or,
have just been in fellowship with
your king.*

*Archaeologists have just un-covered
the stones these builders trod,
Its funny that we should care
how well worn away they be,
as if we need proof of
their first eleven centuries.*

xii

*The Choristers Medal is presented
"for perseverance",
a hand you down to be returned
should you ever leave,
earned for good attendance and
due diligence.*

*The priest lays his hands in blessing
on a faithful soldier and servant
who is now commended and a little
disciplined, and who deserves
the confirmation that he has learnt*

the spirit if not yet the lessons of

catechism. In a year or so the Bishop
will say the blessing, touch his head.
The ring he wears will tap softy, only
this boy will realise that a very gentle
soul has affirmed a calling already

knocking around in his head.

Had he the gift of prophecy
the bishop would have
taken just a little
of the sparkle from his eye.

xiii

A hop, a skip and a jump
hanged his friend
from a tree

and never more or since
did the boy feel the
terror

as he sat miles away
knowing only
the direction of his
fear.

He left prayer hanging
a pendulum un-swung
the course of two years.

They cut his friend down.
He cut his church dead.
The light in his eyes died.

He walked the woods
amidst the quick
and the seriously
the seriously
un-ready dead.

Part Two

*'Defend us Lord
from all perils and dangers
of this night,
as the shades lengthen
and the evening comes'.*

*Give a shadow a name
then say the prayer again
and say it until you see
the face smiling freely.*

*And if it will not smile
God and terror are aligned
in that dread image, attitude
that denies sleep to the sleeper,*

*denies rest to the weary
innocence and peace.
That denies thrice before the*

cock crows.

*And if then the shadow laughs
in dire and fearful imagining
seek not to know the quality of
faith, your ghosts believe in you.*

*Now you must teach them their place
until they forget to disturb the peace,
until God –un-hidden, emerges from
the depths of a shadows' desperate prayer:*

'Lighten our darkness, Lord we pray.

xv

He had to walk through town to piano lessons,
passed a church with a Roman wall.
He would go in and explore as the busses
ran at times which left an hour to kill
and most of all it was warm.

Before long he was turning pages
as a maestro played Bach and soon
he was in his first procession as
tenor, no longer a boy at all.

Not that he would receive communion,
He would wear the badge but not enlist
in the ranks of the faithful who could
bear to touch their living God.

Perhaps his priest thought him pious,
or wondered at the dullness of his eyes.
Death warmed up, singing Sumsion
like an angel, suitably attired.

'They that go down to the sea in ships.
These men see the works of the Lord...
stagger like a drunken man, reel to and fro
and cry unto the Lord in their distress.'

The music mimics the flowing waves
it rises, and falls and falls so softly
that even the storm becomes a whisper
and great waters are quietly released.

xvi

The Body of Christ
is a piece of bread.
Blood of Christ
is a wine, red.

*There is more joy and pain
in earth and heaven
than can be expressed
in the giving or leaving
of this wafer thin bread.*

*When first he took communion next,
shafts of sunlight lit the table set
and he forgot to open his book to sing
until a friend nudged him to begin*

*"let all mortal flesh keep silence
and with fear and trembling stand"*

xvii

*Christ looked along the table,
to see who was out of step,
who would betray him?*

*If the message has changed,
who would want to
shoot the messenger?*

Who was feeling betrayed?

Best examine their feet.

*Who would stick an
angry toe in the water
and then explain why?*

*How we mistrust humility!
Leaders are supposed to lead
and enjoy the fruits,
not offer to do the washing up!*

*Christ blessed their feet.
Disciples must travel*

*they need clean hands
and clean feet.*

*They could not understand
just offered lame excuses.
Perhaps Christ even smiled,
How we love to see as little...
xvii*

*A college party
Talking Heads and girls
in dimly lit corners...*

*Angels of God
and he alone
are counting the*

ways of being afraid

of Jesus Christ

so the song, follows

*who cares the price we pay.
it our little secret and were
never never going...*

*Talking heads and girls
got in the way,
rhythms and heartbeats
dimly lit forays.*

*Angel of love
took him along
took him away.*

He was not alone.

xviii

'Mr Jones put a wiggle in your stride
Mr Jones in back'

If there was sunshine in the valley
there was also frost and fog at night,
the walk back from the valley was long
his second hand coat had half-sown holes.

Huddersfield is hilly, not little hills but
valleys that slope and slide quite keenly;
the Pennine rise up and rise up again.
In such a place, no wonder men sing.

The place is too big to paint with colour
but the valleys carry right well, sound,
be it "Roxanne" at midnight in term-time
or the Hallelujah of the veritable chorus.

'he is a nature boy, think what you like,
this is really where it's at'; there was
sunshine in the valley, rain and fog in places
and in the , the south, bands of high pressure.

In those first years stored up his ghosts,
the shadows in the houses walked past;
Hears the whispers of our moments
in every full drawn curtain and to let sign.

This is where it's at, whilst he remains
his ghosts are not whistling alone.

xix

If the nightingales sing in Deptford
it's a different London Town.
Above the rumble of the tube
and the dockland cranes
the nightingales would sing the blues

never uplifting human hearts again.

*It's a place to spend a summer though,
not quite, the sea in ships, but
from every train pours forth
every kind of man, women and child.*

*Always in hurry, always in a bustle
the bigness of it makes every step
worth less in the overall journey.
He would watch them, idling - sort of
working, sort of playing, the long vacation.*

*He volunteered to be the arms and legs
of two folk who are now at rest,
walked with them for a while
and learn't that people always*

asked him why the broken smile.

*He would sit, swingings conkers beneath a tree,
drinking barley wine through straws
until he could hardly see. Why do people
always ask others why the broken smile?
Why do nightingales sing, in Berkley square?
xx*

*He went to the rocky horror picture show
with his fellow churchmen.*

*Ang' Soc partook in fetish
delighting the Bishop in the Car Park
His inspection of the Chaplains' flock
just more than slightly revealing!*

*The Bishop he took it mildly,
not exactly a stranger
to wearing silly frocks.*

xxi

'After supper he took the cup'
the cannon would intone.
After service he took to sup
with the choir and curate
mimicking the sing song voice
but always wondering
how he himself would sound.

xxii.

The cannon shot him a quizzical frown,
'God is calling you,
 it's a big thing you're saying?'
'Wait until you've earned your gown,
go out into the world, my boy
then I'll throw the real grenades.'

Xxii – removed.

xxiv

"Zacheus was a very little man
and a very little man was he
he climbed up into a sycamore tree
for his saviour he wanted to see

and when his saviour past that way
he looked up into that tree
and said now Zacheus you come down
for I'm coming to your house for tea".

(Sunday School Hymn for the very young).

She would come to tea with candles,
a nineteen fifties fridge giving class
to an otherwise wise hidden kitchen
from which his housemates had been

given to know it was their evening off.

Vege-mince, ginger and guiness
were the only ingredients he cared for,
she would smile politely but then
the eating merely came before

an evening with two wine glasses
reading Larkin, Elliot and his latest
thoughts on whether a glass is
just a rim on the surface or blasted.

She would look at him, and he'd smile
inter-subjectively sipping, passing time.

xxv

"... and I feel that when I am near you
its right.....

The song bird listens
as if he knows the score
and I love you, I love you
like never before."

(Fleetwood Mac)

She washed his feet once
just a bowl and started
saying,he looked so shattered.

He fell asleep where he sat.
She put a blanket on the sofa,
and left him to his dreams.

She told him later that he
murmered thanks, but wondered
who was the person he named.

He suggested it was Stevie Nix?
She said that in future Fleetwood Mac
could take care of washing his socks.

Xxvi – Removed

xxvii

An advert for Chaplains reads

'He died for them,
could you serve them'

Apply to,
The MOD.

He wonders how
soldiers defend their faith?

In penance visits a war memorial
and reads up on his Sassoon.

Remembers his baptismal vow
'continue his faithful soldier and servant'
and how on Church Lad's Brigade Sundays he sang
'At the name of Jesus, every knee shall bow'.

Decides to re-write the advert

'They'll die for you,
can you serve them'.

Wonders how many
grenades chaplains had
lobbed at them to test
their trumpet calling.

If I remember right
I felt it my duty

*Not sure I can ever know
The strength some duties
Call.*

But I can at least remember.

xxviii

*He writes the Chaplains Obituary
for the University Times
not that he died, just passed on
like so many others
when he has served his*

time. 'Time is an anathema'

*One term a fresher, a year, a returner
two, a job hunter and three, a graduate.*

*Don't stay too long he said,
his chronicler knowing only the
loneliness of five making each
new intake a fresh mob of strangers.*

*'He will be missed' with the pain
of those who endure the watching
of the onset of permanence.*

*The copy hits the streets running
the Chaplain seemed almost overcome
at the quality of his passing,
'wrote me up well, did the lad'*

*It falls to those that continue to ensure
the quality of endings, a bright conclusion.
Time makes anathemas, people who by the day
learn to count the missing, fearing the action
end up haunting their ghosts, young men grey.*

xxix

St Paul was a wily old bird
just take the book of Philemon,
runaway slave to save, so he
writes about anying but, but

that's later, tucked in at the end,
no he butters up old Philemon with
how much better it is to be praised!
St Paul was a wily old bird

but to make a point you write a tome?
No, call it a letter and while the reader may frown
he will make reply that is fitting. Old St Paul
could plan a mission, wily as a fox, and worldly.

Xxx Removed

xxxi

There is madness in the village
she catches the bus to town.
Sits top deck, shouting about
the price of sausages and lip stick.

She is perhaps, seventy? Who knows?
No one but her doctor, if it's in her notes?
She asks him if he knows her Bill at Sainsbury's
He would be about his age, she wonders

if he knows that there was trouble at mill
in nineteen fifty three, all burn't down.
Lost her Sam she did, gave her pills,
still takes them, sure you don't know Bill?

There is sadness in the village
a hearse creeps through the town.
From top deck I see it with no motorcade
If Bill is busy at the checkout, I shall have

to ask him the price of bangers, or bite my lip.

xxxii

The morning stars sang together
    and all angels shouted for joy
Have you ever given orders to the morning
    or shown the dawn its place?
(Job 31, 7 & 12)

I would not presume
to tell God his place
although he occasionally
tells me mine.

Let the mornings shine
the proud waves bow
Let the dawn be announced
by the bird song calling 'now'

bring on the dawn,
it is time, it is time
to take our place
in the order of the day.

We would not presume
to pick up the crumbs
from under your table.

But we give you thanks
for our creation and
a voice to sing your praise.

From time to time.

xxxiii

*He was led like a lamb to the
slaughter
  and as sheep before her shearers is
          silent
so he did not open his mouth.
(Isaiah 53, 7)*

*A rolling stone turned over some pebbles
to reveal the remnants of a sickly meal,
the smell was enough to turn a stomach.
The evidence was clear to see.*

*He waited for the tide to wash it clean
but the gulls simply moved the meal
to share with the ganets later,
the scavengers tore it apart.*

*A naturalist filmed it for telly
played it in the common rooms
where all and sundry wondered
how he hadn't noticed the kill.*

*He gave up beach combing soon after
the smell haunted him and even though
the big cats that prey by night were strangers
people always think the kittens had eaten too.*

*Now he sits and licks his fur,
sits in front of fire, contented.
Ponders the life that will
never be again.*

*No one that was ever feline
can ever be perfect...*

*innocent or unaware of the hunter
that beckons in shadows to the game
where the sharp sighted pounce on
the mouse, or the fish, or the vole.*

The beach had been a noble hunt

every day a fresh challenge where
the pride was easy and playful
until the fat cats got greedy

took more than their share
of the manna provided,
brought down the wrath

of dogs and worse, the camera
the man who talks from his eyes.

xxxiv

Emptiness is a vessel that has been full
never mind half measures, all is gone.
The elixir was sweet, powerful like honey
the taste was exciting, left you feeling fizzy.
But that is in the past, there is no more

unless it can be refilled, if you can find
a purveyor of fullness, of purpose, of life.
If you can find one stock up well
for the shelf life is limited and

with every passing year the brand
gets less and less in fashion.
Emptiness is not really a vessel
that has been full, it is the moment
when forgotten, will never be opened at all.

xxxv

On the Falmouth Ferry
I met a girl who once I knew,
three years and a new boyfriend
and half an hour to kill.

Would she talk to him

or would she talk to me
or would she include him
with so little time between

being forgotten and
one more encounter.

The motion was lively
soaking us with spray
making us laugh and
giving us something
new to say,

       until we

disembarked, resumed
our separate ways.

Her name I think was Susan
but I'm not sure, even to this day.

xxxvi

An angel can only hide in heaven
a devil in any crowd
for he wears

the colours of the moment
the expression of the mood
the footwear of the road
and looks only at the
traffic lights to ensure
that he is in step with

every passing soul
that must remain
un-aware of him.

Hell stalks the streets
as silent as the soldier

that takes terror in his sights
and as noisy as the marchers
that wish to reclaim the right

to put evil in its place
and all the while the
devils walking the
broad walks, the
avenues, the
highways,
roads.

Catch a devil on his own

and look him in the eye
and he will sell you
toothpaste or insurance
or perhaps a Hoover bag.

All he has to do is wait
for the followers of fashion
to enter his mall, arcade,
searching for a bargain
or perhaps, just an
indulgence or lampshade.

Angels never sell you
anything,
only the devil has
anything to trade.

The devil is a
store detective.
Eventually you'll pay.

xxxvii

layers, layers, layers,
there is a rule in music
never repeat above three,
consecutively.

You must build up,
alter, transpose,
counter the point
and most of all

never double a octave
or even a fifth
if you want to pass
your music GCSE.

Balls.

Bach is dead.

But lay it on thick
just to prove that
by the age of eighteen
the board can ensure that
originality is

layered in rests.

xxxviii

   ... tender green shoots
like grass sprouting on a roof
         scrorched before it grows up
Isaiah 37, 27

They hadn't time
to take things slowly
he had only the days
allowed for in his suitcase,
by the time he needed laundry

*he would be five hundred
miles away.*

*He was never going back
they both new that.
He un-packed his clothes
into a bin bag
filed her phone number
in his phone book with*

*the photos from the booth
the day they pretended to be
Laurel and Hardy, Sons of the Desert,
singing 'blue ridge mountains,
on the trail of the lonesome pine'.*

*Way out west of the fringe
they played out their booking
for just a week one summer.
Who? Where? When? Don't ask,
it was a one performance show.*

xxxix

*They walked a disused railway
thanking Dr Beeching for his cuts
that would shorten the distance
between x and y coordinates...*

*His companion was a parson
the map from an oxfam shop
laudable and when printed
their route was clearly marked.*

*Only the seeds were now saplings
and the saplings now full trees,
the grass a briered savannah
and un-passable it seemed.*

*It does not do to cross
un-bidden a farmers' fields*

*their walkways are their own
and their privacy means*

*that it was time to re-trace their steps,
-although not quite thirty nine-
but back to where their path left
the road that was still a line.*

*With a map it is easy to know
just how far back you should go
otherwise ask directions from
those who trust not ghosts*

*to chart a course through
the passage of time and place.
They seldom know the obstacles
that the living really face.*

*Dr Beeching cut the railways
but who let the saplings grow?
Those who make their paths redundant
should not really seek to know.*

*Is it really to late to reclaim the track?
Are the bridges burnt and bust?
If they ever did restore this back
would there be diesels or even trucks?*

*After a detour, they wandered back
to their guest house, re-calling
discussions from childhood when
all seemed easy, straightforward and good.*

*Being brothers they argued, being
brothers they called at a book shop
and both bought different maps.*

*Tomorrow's ramble would follow
today's rights of ways.
xl*

Set a marble running
and it will roll down a hill
until it hits a kerb and stops.

Only by the time it hits bottom
it may be more than slightly chipped
by the bumps and scrapes and shocks

and dull and listless no longer be
the bright eyed toy that was
the best of the bunch to be picked.

In fact, may not be worth
retrieving at all.

Better for the marble
to be played against a mate
every dents an honour
that recalls a battle spent

playing a game with rules
until the games outgrown
and the marbles stored
in a box marked
treasures to be given

to the next generation of
youth.

xli

A Rain Drop

Always the colour
that it is set against,
clearly it was intended
to naturally blend in.

Except of course the rainbow,
answering the call

*of the binding spells
that pattern all.*

*The magic is usually in the
ending, that moment when
a splash, a circle, a flower
or even mud is simply changed*

*into a substance refilled.
A possibility regained.*

xlii

*How shall we please those that made us?
When we are little it is easy to please
if we speak nicely, do our dishes
and avoid fighting with jimmy the
one who tears shirts just to tease.*

*A little older, there's home-work to do
and done before we ask to have fun.*

*The older we become the more nearly our
children take up the yoke of being
pleasing to gentler and gentler folk.*

*Had we world enough and time
this need to please would be no
less than ploy to find a line
with which to make a play*

*for the pleasantries that keep us
when we worry that tomorrow
will bring our cares more clearly
to occupy the stillness of the day.*

*Children are bright little things
they shine without a thought
to the pleasure they bring
just by being, being just, young.*

By the time they're grand, we've time
to appreciate them more,
Its our turn to share the fun.

xliii

G K Chesterton once wrote,
spare me those who cherish
their inner light, who won't
look beyond themselves for
a light to shine in the darkness.

For old G K the pre-Christians
appear to have wandered round
covering their heads with lamp shades.

Neither did he think much cop
of those who wandered round
calling the Sun or Moon their pop.

The sun blisters ants and
the moon is cold and damp,
cruelty at play, apparently.

So what of Wooster,
what would he say?
Well, God's a big sort of chap,
suppose I'll have to meet him one day.

Jeeves, not the one to soak up glory
would no doubt arrange a bed time story
for "brother-Sir", a tale of a lighthouse
keeper who beams his light into fog.

Having got it off his Chesterton
Wooster would don eye patches in order
to ensure he could leave the bally light on.

xliv

*There's a leaf softly falling
torn and tossed from its' place
Would that it could, it cannot
fall hard, fall jagged, fall rough,
no, a leaf falls only softly for
it is not heavy enough*

*to be dramatic or denting,
take with it anything larger
than a spider, sleeping,*

sheltered in its bed.

*The leaf is thinly veined
already dead.*

*The spider hangs by a thread
to light to be bent
as the ground hits its head.*

*Not even a leaf
falls without
impact,
ghosts
twitching upon the call*

*of redundant
tracings.*

xlv

*The fires that burn
are smokeless now,
the man with sacks
cannot bring his truck
laden with the coal
that creates any muck.*

*The tenement rows
terraced street by street*

*do not blacken now, and
it is safe to hang out the
washing, save it greets,*

*the clouds of whatever
else might blow in today.
No doubt the place smells
cleaner, in a no smell way.*

*The houses have been dusted
with a sand blasters hose,
all nicely coloured with
a facia devoid of spoils.*

*The fires that burn
come from showrooms now.
Mdf fireplaces effect
to glow and keep
us cosy in odourless
comfy slippered rooms
watching cookery shows.*

Finally

He was I
I remember he
but only those now
know me.

Lest they forget.

Notes on Steps

The first draft of steps, yes, forty-five poems in a series in the order here presented was written over seven consecutive evenings, an admission which perhaps comparison with Trollopes' frenetic endeavours. Such a comparison would however miss the point as in fact there are times when a series is in your head just waiting for the moment to pop out.

So it was with 'Holy Island' and 'The Cathedral'. I have for the last couple of years found that poems come in groups, even when the subject matter is diverse.

The poem is in one sense biographical and in other senses fictional in that it re-writes history to make a point or to protect identity; my views on privacy are fully explained in the notes on "No Way to Feed a Flock".

Notes on specific sections.

xi: See "Bamburgh Castle is high and tall: 'Holy Island'.

xiii   The first part of this was written in sequence, the second added the evening after I completed xli. This is course takes for its' text one of the two collects that are said at every service of evening prayer (or evensong). "The perils and dangers of this night" is one of the most evocative phrases in the prayer book. In the dark time described, this prayer was for a while full of the possibilities this poem describes, and then and since, a part of the healing process.

xxvi   say. At the end of the day I slogged for exams; they serve a purpose whilst they continue to exist.

xxxv: Perhaps her name was Susan, perhaps not: I almost never discuss the identities of people, real or imagined in poems. See: "Privacy Laws' in 'No Way to Feed a Flock.

xxxvi   When posting this online in a poets private internet forum for comment, shortly after the terrible events at the World Trade Centre in New York, I was at pains to stress that no critical sentiments were being expressed here. 'Trade' here is a metaphor and should not be taken literally: there is no biblical exhortation against honest trade, although history is replete with different interpretations of Gospels comments on money, wealth, etc.

xxxix   Is almost apocryphal. My elder brother and I are happy to confirm that we have been caught out by such a map on such a walk, although many years ago. The poem portrays a possible version of events, if not the actual.

xl   The link in this poem is the reference to rules.

xli   Is the only poem with a title. It would not work without one and it is too important as a bridge between the emptiness of the preceding poems and what follows to omit. It is also the only poem in the series to focus on a single object in this way. In the loosest possible sense, it also seemed right to maintain a suggestion of a sonnet.

Commentary : 2001.

Note: 2014.

At a gathering of poets I happened to mention that I had once written over forty poems in a week and this caused some astonishment and not a little incredulity. I went on to explain that that which was written in a week, has taken well over a decade to edit and has had to wait years more before I would agree to publish it.

Write in haste, repent at leisure! Edit forever!

Even now, it is necessarily published incomplete as parts of it remain personal, to be shared only with the closest of friends, past and present.

The Universe unfolds as it should

The stars are all old
and beyond the reach of time
for it is only their echoes we see.

Their stories are all told
and beyond the reach of time
for only their echoes meet thee.

In the eye of my mind
I behold, each moment,
now, never, forever,
and the instant is lost
to wonder at the smallness
of this one mortal, me.

The stars are all old
and beyond the reach of time
and will I hope be everlasting
and with that in mind
I wish them to be
the very last thing
I see.

Frieth Parish Church

The door is open, a key holder is not required
and heavy, solid, and opens slowly, on ancient
hinges, still oiled. Its petty, even pace belies
my need for haste, my time being short, today.
Thus, un-hurried I, pass into the gates of Him,
even, with due effort, I enter into the House of the Lord.

The church is smaller than recollection would have it,
for I have passed this way before, in sorrow, as a child
My Grandparents lie buried in the ground outside,
their names newly adorn stones I have photographed.
I find my place of old, kneel and offer my silent prayers,
alone and undisturbed within these well remembered walls.

"Peace be with them that die in the Lord"
I repeat the legends, I add my own new words,
for although my repertoire of prayers is not small
every day brings new blessings for which I give thanks.
Every passing brings home to me, blessings for which I give thanks,
The door is placed gently home; such rest eternal grant unto them.

2000

NOTES

The poem 'Prove all things, hold fast to that which is good', was a runner up in the 2001 Manchester Cathedral Religious Poetry Competition and published by Manchester Cathedral in accordance with the rules of that competition in their anthology. The judge of that competition was, Archbishop Dr Rowan Williams, then Wales, subsequently Canterbury.

On writing religious poetry: A brief essay.

There is only one Schubert capable of arranging Ave Maria, or perhaps, there is only Schubert and Mozart. There is only one Bob Dylan capable of writing Mr Tambourine Man with his skipping reels of rhyme. Abiding in the vine is simply not a guarantee that you can write a book of psalms (which should be the impossible ambition of any decent religious poet).

Every young poet writes about love. Of course and why not? Every young religious poet has a tendency to see angels in the architecture and even the writers of Dr Who have managed to make angels weep.

The religious poet must combine both the practise of faith, and his or her insight into what is believed. The sounds, the smells, the touch, the sense must be evoked, as they are in many religious services. What has gone before, what is tradition, what is familiar must be approached with the question, what is perhaps relevant to something that happened today. It is ok to re-invent, for all art inspired by faith is a revelation; an expression of some insight that is worth daring to share.

But religious poetry is not a vocation in itself.

Writing religious poetry can easily become an almost monastic pursuit. To pray, to reflect, to seek meaning is a discipline enshrined in most forms of priestly and lay discipleship. Rightly so. But, except you are in an order devoted entirely to prayer, in the world, but almost completely outside of it, as a poet your writing should reflect the world as it is. All of it. The good, the bad and the ugly, to plagiarise that film title.

I can write religious poetry, because I can feel the flow of faith around me, not just from my own tradition but from others and from other faiths. I can do so because I can write about love, about hate, about poverty, about hope, beauty and so much more. I dare, I dare, I dare, and I occasionally dare to gently touch upon things I hold dear, like Cathedrals and Holy Island.

In doing so I can be gentle, or even angry. I can call out a doctrine or even a saint who seems to need a new dentist! What I cannot do is stop writing poems about the rest of life, even damning cauliflower cheese to its deserved perdition because religious poetry is the most difficult subject I address.

If you want to write religious poetry, great, but, sit in a cathedral for a couple of hours, or on a hillside, and see what happens. The Holy Spirit will I imagine forgive me for saying that he is an awkward so and so and I can wait months, or even years between a decent religious poem coming along. Actually, I would never claim that inspiration as anyone who does is perhaps missing the point: Poets invite us to ask questions, ask us to consider whether our experiences are shared or worth seeking for. Poets should not I think seek to preach, they encourage you to ask, to receive, to be open to experience. My favourite poet, Larkin, would ask you to consider:

Our almost-instinct almost true:
What will survive of us is love

However, Miss Joan Hunter Dunn might not agree. She would be too busy writing about tennis players who should spend more time on the courts than courting their own fantasy: Even if their tennis partner was summoned by those eternal and mystical bells. A whiskey priest or poet knows when to play and when to take, a shot. Love all, or deuce. Religious poetry may enjoy the benefits of completion, or peer review, but, of its' nature, it is the least suited to such judgements. Except of course where it regardless of your faith, inspires good works.

Religious poetry should ultimately seek to inspire, even if that is only possible by achieving a balance between work that is full of fear and doubt, and work that is confident of a bright conclusion. In other words, it is ok to follow in the footsteps of writers like C.S Lewis, if you know where you are going. If you fail to offer hope, which Lewis of course did offer, you should question why you are writing. Of course life is hard, but we poets at different times must balance the nursery rhymes with the loneliness of clouds. We must live, and of course, let live. True poetry should be accessible to those of your own faith, other faiths, or none.

It should capture the wonder of being, without dictating what that must be. Perhaps you can wonder what might be, being wonderful.

Daniel Janes 2014

Advertisement

O tempora O mores!

A short collection for Advent by Daniel Janes

ISBN-10: 1502790629

ISBN-13: 978-1502790620

Available in print and for Kindle on Amazon.

The Tale of the Christmas Rabbit.

The snow fell, drifting slow, drifting slowly
against the fence, down below, well below me
Halfway up it, lamplight glistening, a rabbit stood
with shining eyes, sugar frosted coat, it   coldly stood.

Good King Wenceslas looked out, not I
the snow laying deeply, crisply, evenly
his breath on the window pain, misting
that rabbit, sugar coated and glistening.

In the morning the rabbit was gone,
nothing to show where he had shone
I asked my mummy to put some carrots out
to fill the tummy of a long eared runabout.

The snow fell, drifting slow, drifting slowly
against the fence, down below, well below me,
Halfway up it, lamplight glistening, a rabbit stood
with shining eye, sugar frosted coat, it   nibbling stood.

Huddersfield.
for Christmas 2000

Printed in Great Britain
by Amazon.co.uk, Ltd.,
Marston Gate.